# NFU LEGAL GUIDE

# FARM-GATE SALES TO THE PUBLIC

## Second Edition

# NFU Legal Guide

# FARM-GATE SALES TO THE PUBLIC

## SECOND EDITION

**Shaw & Sons Ltd**
**Shaway House, Bourne Road,**
**Crayford, Kent DA1 4BZ**

While the publishers and the NFU have taken every care in preparing the material included in this book, any statements made as to the legal or other implications of particular actions are made in good faith purely for general guidance and cannot be regarded as a substitute for professional advice. Consequently, no liability can be accepted for loss or expense incurred as a result of relying in particular circumstances on statements made in this book.

First Edition 1987
Second Edition 1991

ISBN 0 7219 1081 5

Printed in Great Britain by Bell and Bain Ltd., Glasgow

# Contents

Foreword

Acknowledgment

Introduction

1. General aspects
   1.1 Personal skills and resources
   1.2 Researching the market
   1.3 Financial considerations
   1.4 Promotion
   1.5 Insurance

2. Legal requirements
   2.1 Town and country planning
   2.2 Advertisements and signs
   2.3 Building control
   2.4 Sale of Goods Act 1979
   2.5 Consumer Protection Act 1987
   2.6 Food Safety Act 1990
   2.7 Hygiene
   2.8 Weights and measures
   2.9 Labelling and advertising of food
   2.10 Health, safety and welfare of employees
   2.11 Safety of visitors
   2.12 Shop closing hours
   2.13 Sunday trading
   2.14 "Pick-your-own" selling
   2.15 Rating

3. Appendices
   Appendix I: Acts and regulations
   Appendix II: Sources of further advice and information

Index

# Foreword

The NFU's legal guide FARM-GATE SALES TO THE PUBLIC was published in 1987, the first of a series of advisory books for farmers and growers published with Shaw & Sons.

Producers are showing a growing interest in diversifying into new farming enterprises. Direct selling can provide one source of extra income. But developing a new enterprise can present new and unfamiliar problems, in particular the legislation affecting dealings with the general public.

This second edition sets out to assist the producer by making him/her aware of the legal requirements on aspects ranging from planning through to labelling and rating. It is a vital addition to the farm office of anyone contemplating a direct selling venture.

The book has been produced in conjunction with the Farm Shop and Pick Your Own Association, the principal producer organisation involved in direct selling activities which has given the book its full backing.

C. D. Naish
President, NFU

# Acknowledgment

The NFU would like to acknowledge the help of Bridget Hamilton, Sarah Thodey, Clive Black, Xanthe Neale and Jane Connor.

# Introduction

As farmers and growers embrace diversification as a chance to achieve greater profit, direct selling enterprises can certainly work for some. Generally, direct selling can be carried out from a farm shop, or a pick your own service. It could also be in the form of a farm stall, garden centre or even a craft shop.

However, if the venture is to succeed, it is vital that the producer has the right personal skills, can promote his/her business, gets to know the local demand and understands the legal aspects.

The aim of this book is to guide a new venture through the initial stages. It does not pretend to be a comprehensive synopsis of all aspects of farm-gate sales, rather a reference point giving suggestions and names of professional advisors whose advice should be sought.

Part 1 of this book looks briefly at personal skills, research, promotion and financial considerations. Part 2 is the guide to the more important legal requirements and regulations covering retail sales of agricultural produce. If you are in any doubt about how the regulations apply to you, reference should be made to the statutes and the regulations themselves. A list of the more important of these is given in Appendix 1.

You must also check with your local authority and Trading Standards Officer whether there are any by-laws or local acts covering food shops, food sales and roadside selling, ensuring that these regulations are complied with. If in any doubt, consult the local authority or seek legal advice.

In Part 3 you will find the appendices which include a useful list of organisations providing further information and assistance.

We wish you luck in your venture.

# 1. General aspects

## 1.1 Personal skills and resources

You must be able to deal with the general public if your direct selling enterprise is to be a success. Naturally any retailing flair you may possess will be an added bonus. In addition it is important to decide whether you mind having people wandering around your farm or arriving at almost any time during the day. Also it may be necessary to have the ability to produce a wide range of crops as customers are unlikely to be attracted if you only sell one or two products.

Whether members of your family are able to help is also an important consideration in these enterprises. Many existing farm shops would fail if they relied totally on employed labour. You will also need to find out if any local part or full-time staff can be recruited.

Your location is also a vital aspect. You need to be fairly and easily accessible from a motorway or main road, and provide adequate car-parking facilities, all of which could give you an advantage over local High Street shops.

## 1.2 Researching the market

Whatever the enterprise you are considering there is a fundamental need for some basic research. Market research is arguably the most important stage of the development of a successful business operation as it determines whether there is a market opportunity. It is no good supplying something which doesn't fit the demand. The main considerations for local market research include:

(a) the catchment area – from how far afield are customers likely to come?
(b) size of population in that area
(c) social class

1

(d) ages and size of typical families
(e) means of transport

Before committing yourself, you must also find out who your competitiors are and consider whether you can compete on cost, quality, service, or some other unique aspect. Once you have some idea of your own strengths and weaknesses, you will be able to create the right kind of business, so as to make it as effective as possible.

Special care must be taken to make sure that there are not already enough local suppliers – as is the case with farm shops or pick-your-own enterprises in some areas.

So how do you go about researching your market? Start by talking to people – not competitors and potential customers. Also seek out possible sources of advice. Appendix II lists out some useful contacts. You may also like to try your local Small Firms Service, Chambers of Commerce, and Enterprise Agencies. They may also be able to help you build up a picture of the nature of the local market. The Library may also have useful population and market research information. Local press, Yellow Pages, trade and special interest magazines can also be useful.

If possible it is a good idea to try out your venture on a small scale first. In the case of a farm shop this can be done by using an existing building rather than investing heavily in any conversions or new buildings. Take note of any "feedback" from your customers and try to use it to influence your pricing, product range, shop layout, etc.

## 1.3 Financial considerations

Good profits can be achieved from direct selling – particularly where the enterprise is well run and has built up a reputation for freshness, taste, flavour or some other quality such as the wholesome, country-food image.

Retail margins can be anything up to 100%, especially where the product cannot easily be found elsewhere as in the case of organically produced vegetables. Pick-your-own enterprises tend to compete mainly on price with other local outlets, and therefore you need to pitch prices between the wholesale and retail level. It is important to allow for wastage and loss of weight in setting prices for the farm shop.

The gross profit target will depend to a certain extent on fixed overheads – you should aim for around 10% profit (before tax).

Grants are available from MAFF for setting up a farm shop under the farm diversification scheme. The grant covers 25% of the cost of capital expenditure up to £35,000, thus the maximum sum available to an enterprise is £8,750. Grants should be applied for through local MAFF offices. In certain circumstances the Rural Development Commission may also be able to offer grant aid. For more detailed information please contact your local RDC office.

## 1.4 Promotion

Good promotion of your venture is vital. Advertising is merely selling in print. It is easy to be persuaded to waste large sums of money for little return. But if cash is wisely spent on planned advertising (as a set percentage of budgeted sales turnover) the results should be rewarding. Remember also there is no point generating a demand which you cannot satisfy. Guidance on what claims for your products you can and cannot make can be obtained from the Advertising Standards Authority Ltd., Brook House, Torrington Place, London WC1E 7HN (071 580 5555).

Specifically for farm shops selling meat is the MLC/NFU Getting Results For Farm Shops brochure available from NFU, Membership Services, 4 St. Mary's Hill, Stamford, Lincolnshire PE9 2DP.

Well designed advertisements are by far the most effective and it may be worth getting a professional designer to prepare the artwork for you. Students at a local college could also be approached for much less cost. The Department of Trade and Industry also have a Design Advisory Service which provides consultancy on all aspects of product design, including packaging and promotional literature. Further details can be obtained from the Design Council, 28 Haymarket, London SW1 5SU (071 839 8000).

There are many opportunities for good public relations. If anything newsworthy happens to you or your company – then let the local newspaper or radio know about it by ringing the news desk. Even the news that you have started a new business may gain coverage. Direct mail shots or circulars to the public are another way of promoting your company. The post office can offer a direct mailshot service at favourable rates for new businesses.

Another important aspect of promotion, particularly in the case of farm shops, is shop layout. The shop must be bright, clean and attractive. It is better to aim for a rural or country image rather than a mini-supermarket. Professionally produced signs are also a further promotional tool. The legal aspects of signs and advertisements are considered in section 2.2.


# 1.5 Insurance

Every farmer and horticulturalist should have insurance which protects his livelihood. For example, the buildings should be insured against fire and other events, liability for injury to employees must be insured against (this is compulsory) and liability to third parties should also be covered. So, why should a move into direct selling require you to reconsider your existing insurances?

First and foremost, it is essential that the insurances clearly cover this new activity. Some policies may apply to only farming activities and it is not certain whether retail sales fall within this description. So it is most important that you advise your insurers of buildings, produce, live and deadstock and vehicles concerned with the new activity.

Secondly, you should, with professional help from your NFU Group Secretary, carefully go through your existing insurances and establish where new items need to be insured, e.g. a Portacabin, shop stock, cash, and so on, depending on the precise nature of your enterprise.

Thirdly, again in conjunction with your insurance adviser,

consider whether new risks now require insurance protection. If the new venture takes off and produces a healthy income, that income will need protection: if a farm shop is burnt out your fire insurance will cover the cost of rebuilding but not the loss of revenue during the period when your selling is at a standstill or severely curtailed.

It is impossible to provide a guide that would suit everyone and so the best advice is to consult your NFU Group Secretary about extending existing insurance policies and/or getting extra cover to match the risks of your new venture.

# 2. Legal requirements

## 2.1 Town and country planning

The Town and Country Planning Act 1990 makes all "development" as defined by the Act subject to planning control. Development requires formal planning permission unless specifically exempted. Broadly, development takes two forms: operations – such as building or engineering works – and uses. Development occurs when works are begun or when there is material change of use of land or buildings.

However, under the General Development Order 1988 (the GDO), certain agricultural development is exempt from the requirement to obtain planning permission. Any farmer or grower planning direct sales must therefore decide whether his proposals will involve either building or engineering operations not covered by the General Development Order 1988, or a material change of use.

**Building operations.** Article Three of the General Development Order 1988 effectively grants planning permission for agricultural buildings in the circumstances set out in Schedule Two, Part 6 of the order:

(a) the building must be reasonably necessary for the purposes of agriculture within an agricultural unit of at least one acre (0.4 ha.). "Agriculture" includes horticulture, fruit growing, market gardens and nursery grounds. Separate parcels of land in the same ownership will not be included for the purpose of calculating the size of the unit in question.

(b) the ground area of the proposed new building, together with any other building (except for a dwelling) erected on the holding within 90 m (99 yds) during the previous two years, must not exceed 465 sq.m (5,000 sq.ft).

(c) the height of the building must not exceed 12 m (39 ft) or 3 m (9.8 ft) if within 3 kilometres of an aerodrome.

(d) no part of the building must be within 25 m (82 ft) of the metalled portion of a trunk or classified road. (Some minor roads are classified; information on the status of roads can be obtained from the Highways Department of the County Council.)

**Engineering operations.** These include works such as the laying out of a farm track. The 1990 Act states specifically that they include the formation of a means of access to a highway.

To benefit from the agricultural exemption, engineering operations must, like buildings, be reasonably necessary for the purpose of agriculture within an agricultural unit of more than one acre. There is no limit on the area which such works may take up, but they are subject to the same height restrictions and the distance from roads limitation specified above.

**Removal of permitted development rights.** The local planning authority can issue Article Four Direction, which removes the permitted development rights granted by the General Development Order 1988. Such Direction must be approved by the Secretary of State, who will confirm them only when he considers that the type of development permitted by the GDO would cause a specific threat to the amenity of an area. A Direction may cover a single holding or may apply over a larger area of the countryside.

An Article Four Direction does not necessarily mean that no development will take place in the area to which it applies. It does mean however that a planning application will be required for an operation which was formerly permitted development under the GDO.

**Material change of use.** Where the agricultural land is subject to a material change of use and is used for purposes which are non-agricultural and which cannot be regarded as ancillary to agriculture, planning permission is required.

Whether or not a change of use amounts to a material change of use is a question of fact and degree which will be decided by the Secretary of State or the courts if there is a dispute. There are therefore no hard and fast rules, but case

## 2 Legal Requirements

law and planning appeals provide guidance on the approach likely to be adopted. The following sections deal with the types of use most likely to be found in a direct sales operation.

### (a) The sale of home-grown produce

The sale from a holding of produce grown on that holding does not normally require planning permission because it is considered to be "ancillary to the agricultural use of the land", in other words to be subsidiary to the main agricultural use.

Therefore a grower does not require planning permisssion to start pick-your-own sales, or to use an existing farm building as a shop for the sale of produce grown on the holding.

The exception to that general rule is home-grown produce which has been substantially altered or adapted for sale (for example, joints of meat, jam, yoghurt etc.). The processes involved in adapting this produce for sale are regarded as above and beyond the minimum necessary to make it saleable. The processing and subsequent sale will involve a "material change of use", particularly if it entails any manufacturing or other process not normally undertaken on the farm. In these circumstances the sale of the produce is no longer regarded as ancillary to the agricultural use of the land.

### (b) Sales of produce not grown on the holding

In planning terms, sales must be ancillary to the agricultural use of the holding on which the produce is grown. Therefore produce from another holding cannot normally be sold without planning permission. This is the case even if the piece of land on which the produce is grown is in the same ownership as the holding on which the farm shop is situated. An exception is made to this rule if the amount of produce brought onto the holding is so small as to be insignificant for the purposes of planning control. There is no fixed rule as to exactly what amount of produce can be brought in from elsewhere. Generally, case histories indicate that approximately five per cent of total sales may well be seen as acceptable.

If the operator of a farm shop owns town holdings which are run separately or are physically separate, it is unlikely that they will be treated as a single planning unit.

The sale of produce from one holding, in a farm shop on the other holding would therefore require planning permission.

## Guidance on specific products.

*(a) Meat.* The slaughter of livestock and the jointing and packaging necessary to prepare meat for sale are not regarded as activities incidental to the agricultural use of land. So meat cannot be sold from the farm without planning permission.

*(b) Poultry.* The position is less clear cut, because the slaughter of poultry tends to be regarded as a normal part of agricultural operations and becuse it is often a highly seasonal activity. The fact that normally no jointing is needed to prepare the produce for sale may also be relevant. The sale of oven-ready, as opposed to New York dressed poultry is more likely to require planning permission because the removal of giblets could be deemed to go beyond the minimum necessary to prepare the bird for sale.

*(c) Fish.* The above comments on poultry apply to some extent to the sale of fish, as it is widely accepted that the sale of fish for the table from an agricultural holding is ancillary to agriculture. Where, however, the fish is caught using rod and line by members of the public, it is likely that this will be regarded as as a material change of use from agriculture to some form of recreational use. Planning permission would then be required.

*(d) Milk.* The preparation of milk for sale to the public will – with the exception of milk served to paying guests – involve pasteurisation. It could be held that this represents the minimum necessary to make the product saleable, but at least one planning appeal has rejected this argument, resulting in the seller of pasteurised and bottled milk having to obtain planning permission.

*(e) Milk products.* If the sale of milk – albeit pasteurised and bottled milk – is conclusively held to need planning permission then the sale of yoghurt, butter and cheese will also need planning permission.

**9**

*( f ) Wine and cider.* In the absence of case law on the sale of wine or cider it is difficult to offer precise guidance, but it seems likely that the wine and cider-making processes would be regarded more as manufacturing than agriculture. The bottling and labelling of either product might also be seen as a use not incidental to agriculture, even though the growing of the grapes or apples would itself be agriculture. Thus the sale of wine or cider will probably require planning consent.

*(g) Vegetables.* Normally home grown vegetables can be sold from the holding without planning permission. However, sales of cooked vegetables – baked potatoes or boiled beetroot for instance – probably require planning consent; similarly, freezing, dicing or slicing are likely to be considered non-agricultural processes and planning permission is required.

*(h) Fruit.* The above advice on vegetables also applies to fruit. Where home-grown fruit is sold in its raw state no planning permission will be required. However, the sale of cooked or processed fruit – perhaps in the form of jams or other preserves – almost certainly would.

**"Growing on" of horticultural produce.** A planning appeal held that plants, shrubs and trees brought on to a holding for resale, and kept there for only a limited time, were not produce of that holding, even though they grew while there. Although in this case it was decided that planning permission was necessary, one should nonetheless look at the individual facts of the case, as there might well be circumstances where it would be valid to argue that "grown on" produce is the produce of the holding. Factors to take into account include:

- The length of time the plants are kept on the holding – the longer the time the stronger the case.
- Do the plants grow significantly in that time or undergo any change in state, e.g. come into flower?
- Are they kept and tended in specialised growing houses or glasshouses or are they merely stored in a convenient area awaiting sale?

- Does "grown on" produce form a substantial part of the produce on the holding?
- Is it an established and commonly employed horticultural practice on holdings in the area?

It is recognised that produce has to be adequately "packed" to make it saleable, and therefore planting out home-grown horticultural produce into pots or containers should be accepted as a normal horticultural operation. However, there is doubt as to whether this includes making up flower decorations in containers, for example hanging baskets. If horticultural produce were adapted in any other way for sale, or not sold as produced, then that operation might require planning permission.

**What to do if in doubt.** Making a material change of use without permission can have serious consequences. A planning authority may serve an enforcement notice to stop the unauthorised use.

There is a right of appeal but it is obviously better to start trading in the secure knowledge that planning permission is not required (or if required, that it has been granted), rather than invest time and money in an enterprise which may be forced to cease after a few weeks.

If there is any doubt as to whether a proposed farm shop needs permission, a letter should be sent to the planning authority asking for a formal ruling on whether or not planning consent must be obtained.

This is known as section 64 determination and is free of charge. In some cases the planning authority will have a form for the purpose but elsewhere you must supply the authority with full details of your proposal, together with any necessary plans. If you believe that permission is not required and the planning authority rule otherwise it is possible to appeal against the authority's determination.

It may save time to apply for planning permission at the same time as requesting a s.64 determination. This means that the planning authority will start to process the planning application whilst considering whether or not permission is in fact required.

## 2 Legal Requirements

**National Parks and other Article 1(6) areas.** Special rules apply in National Parks and certain other areas listed in Article 1(6) of the GDO. Details of any agricultural building which it is proposed to erect as permitted development under the GDO must be supplied to the Park Authority before work is begun. The authority then have twenty-eight days to decide whether they wish to intervene on the questions of the siting, design and external appearance of the building. If they decide to do so, their approval of these matters must be obtained before the building can be erected. This requirement also applies to farm tracks in such areas.

**Planning fees.** An application for planning permission must normally be accompanied by a fee to cover the cost of processing. The planning authority will specify the fee. The fee is not returnable if permission is refused.

If the operations in question would have been permitted development, but for an Article 4 direction removing normal rights, no fee is payable.

The same fee exemption applies to approval of details of buildings or tracks in National Parks (see above).

New buildings for agricultural purposes are also partially exempted from planning fees. The first 465 square metres of floor space is free, fees being paid only on the amount by which that area is exceeded. The concession applies to any building for agricultural purposes built on agricultural land, whether or not the erection of the building qualifies for the GDO exemption. But note that the fees concession operates only if you are seeking full planning permission. It does not apply to applications for outline consent.

A nominal standard fee is charged for planning applications concerning car parks, and service roads and other means of access on land used for a single undertaking, if it is for a purpose incidental to the existing use of the land. For example, the construction of a car park to serve a farm shop which was itself established without the need for planning permission, would be subject to the concessionary fee if it needed planning consent. Where the car park was intended to serve a shop which had needed planning consent – perhaps because it was used for the sale of meat or "imported produce" – the concessionary fee would seem to apply only once the shop was established, and therefore an "existing use". In the absence of case law, however, it is impossible to offer precise guidance. Fees for the display of advertisements are discussed in the following chapter.

**Commentary.** If you do conclude that planning permission is needed, it is useful to talk to the planning officer who deals with your area at an early stage. This will help you to find out whether the authority has particular concerns about the proposal, and what you might do to meet concerns and so make the scheme more acceptable.

Generally planners will wish to be satisfied that access and parking arrangements are adequate and that the local road will be able to accommodate the traffic likely to be attracted to the farm shop. Planners will also be concerned about the visual effect of the development on its surroundings, but against this must balance the need to encourage new enterprises in rural areas.

Central government's planning policy guidance to local authorities encourages the re-use of redundant agricultural buildings, and the planning authority must take this into account even in areas such as Green Belts where especially restrictive policies apply.

Planners should not take into account objections received from local traders since the effect of the new shop on existing retailers is not relevant to the decision.

## 2.2 Advertisements and signs

The display of advertisements and signs is subject to special regulations. They are currently the Town and Country Planning (Control of Advertisements) Regulations 1989. The regulations provide that "deemed consent" is granted for certain types of sign, while others need the "express consent" of the local planning authority (i.e. your district or borough council).

## 2 Legal Requirements

**Exemptions from the need to obtain express consent.**
Deemed consent is granted for, among others, the following
types of sign:

(a) advertisements not exceeding 0.3 square metres in area
displayed for the purpose of identification, direction or
warning with respect to the land or buildings on which
they are displayed. (This permits the display of the name
of the farm but very little else.)

(b) advertisements relating to any person, partnership or
company separately carrying on a profession, business or
trade at the premises where they are displayed; limited to
one advertisement, not exceding 0.3 square metres in area,
in respect of each such person, partnership or company,
or, in the case of premises with entrances on different road
frontages, one advertisement at each of two entrances.
(Such advertisements could be used to display the name
of the business but little else.)

(c) temporary signs announcing a sale of goods or livestock,
and displayed on the land where the goods or livestock
are kept, or where the sales are held, (*not* being land
which is normally used whether at regular intervals or
otherwise, for the purposes of holding such sales) such
signs are limited to one advertisement not exceeding 1.2
square metres in area at each site where they are
displayed. (It may be possible to advertise pick-your-own
sales from a field using signs permitted under this class,
but note that signs must not be on display more than
twenty-eight days before the event or later than fourteen
days after its conclusion.)

(d) advertisements displayed on business premises detailing
the business being carried out, the goods sold, and the
name of the owner. If displayed on the wall of a shop,
that wall must contain a shop window. The sign must not
reach the same height as the bottom of any first floor
window. There is no restriction on size outside an Area of
Special Control (*see below*).

(e) advertisements displayed on the forecourts of business
premises showing details as in paragraph (d) above,
subject to a maximum combined area of 4.5 square

metres. (A shop would be "business premises" but it seems that a pick-your-own area would not.)

(f) advertisements in the form of a flag attached to a single flagstaff fixed in an upright position on the roof of a building. This may bear only the name or device of the person(s) occupying the buildings.

Note that advertisements may not be displayed without express consent if they contain letters, figures, symbols or devices exceeding 0.75 metres in height (less in an Area of Special Control).

Outside Areas of Special Control, the highest point of an advertisement other than a flag advertisement may be up to 4.6 metres from ground level.

The local planning authority has power to order you to take down an advertisement with deemed consent, where they are satisfied that this is necessary to "remedy a substantial injury to the amenity of the locality or a danger to members of the public". This is subject to a right of appeal to the Secretary of State.

The Secretary of State has power to overrule deemed consent to signs in a particular area or case. Where the Secretary of State has made a direction under Regulation 7 of the 1989 Regulations, you must obtain express consent for any class of advertisement to which it applies.

**Areas of special control.** In Areas of Special Control certain types of advertisement may not be displayed at all. Deemed consent is granted for the display of advertisements described in paragraphs (a) to (f) above, but with amendments as follows:

(i) advertisements described in paragraph (d) may occupy no more than one tenth of the total area up to a height of 3.6 metres from ground level of the face of the building on which they are displayed.

(ii) letters, figures and so forth may be no higher than 0.3 metres.

(iii) apart from flag advertisements, to which no height restrictions apply, advertisements may not be displayed above 3.6 metres from ground level.

**Exclusions from control.** The following are outside the scope of the regulations:

(i) advertisements displayed on a vehicle, so long as the vehicle is not used primarily for the display of advertisements. (This would permit the display of advertisements on, say, a working farm lorry but *not* on a redundant cart or tractor, which is no longer "normally employed as a moving vehicle on any highway...".)

(ii) advertisements displayed on balloons flown at a height greater than 60 metres, with no more than one balloon per site, and for no more than ten days in one calendar year (but note that Civil Aviation Authority consent is required before a balloon can be flown higher than 60 metres). The exemption does not apply to the use of balloons in Areas of Special Control, Conservation Areas, National Parks or Areas of Outstanding Natural Beauty.

**Fees for the display of advertisements.** Where a display needs express consent, the application must be accompanied by a fee. The normal fee is reduced when the advertisement is displayed:

(i) in connection with a business at the premises on which it is displayed – for example an advertisement on the wall of a farm shop; or

(ii) as an "advance sign" of premises (such as a farm shop) situated near the proposed advertisement, but not visible from where the sign is to be displayed.

**What to do if in doubt.** The display of advertisements in breach of the 1989 regulations is an offence. It is therefore wise to check with the local planning authority before displaying an advertisement, even where it seems clear that the display would benefit from deemed consent.

**Commentary.** Never have a mass of untidy signs next to the road. They will not impress your potential customers, who, as well as possibly finding the signs difficult to read, may feel that scruffy presentation is a reflection of general low standards. Furthermore untidy signs will not impress passers-by or those living nearby.

The ideal sign is attractive and neat – though it will not necessarily have been prepared by a professional – and contains a simple, easy to read message. Remember that motorists will be able to read very little in the short time that your signs are visible to them; and the higher the speed, the less they will be able to take in.

Consider erecting a sign – prominently stating "Farm Shop" or "Pick-your-Own" – into which you can also slide the names of the main current crops. But resist the temptation to include a long list.

Your local planners should be happy to discuss the merits of your proposals, as well as explaining the legal position.

## 2.3 Building control

The operation and guiding principles of building control differ from those of planning control. Even if erection or conversion of a building does not need planning permission, this does not mean that the work will not need approval under building regulations.

**Erection of new buildings.** A new farm shop building would require approval. You should check with the building control department of your local district or borough council whether "full plans" will be required, or just a "building notice".

**Conversion of existing buildings.** The conversion of an agricultural building for use as a farm shop would, in terms of building control (though not necessarily planning), mean a material change of use. The local authority can advise whether "full plans" would be needed. If not, a building notice should be submitted to the Local Authority (unless an approved inspector is appointed instead – *see below*).

Building inspectors are likely to check the fire precautions, the sturdiness of the structure, and such matters as ventilation, food storage, toilets and heating appliances.

Anyone erecting a new building to be used as a shop will be required to provide access for the disabled, but you are not obliged to provide such access in an existing building converted for use as a shop.

**Approved inspectors.** Under the Building Act 1984 the person carrying out the work can opt for the responsibility of making sure building regulations are followed to be given to an "approved inspector" instead of the local authority. The building control department should be able to supply a list.

**Building control fees.** Where full plans are deposited, fees are paid in two instalments: when plans are first deposited, and when the local authority's inspection has been carried out. Where a building notice is submitted, the fee payable is the sum of the appropriate plan and inspection fees. Fees are calculated according to the cost of the building works.

**Commentary.** Remember that the building control inspector will be mainly concerned with the safety and health of people either using a building or otherwise likely to be affected, by, for example, structural failure. Broadly speaking, the greater the number of people affected the greater the inspector's concern is likely to be. You should not be surprised if the inspector looks very carefully at proposals for a farm shop and is reluctant to relax the requirements of the building regulations.

On the other hand, do bear in mind that the Government advises local authorities *(see for example DoE Circular 8/87 on Historic Buildings and Conservation Areas)* to be "sensible and sensitive" in their use of such regulations if the future of an historic building is at stake.

## 2.4 Sale of Goods Act 1979

Sales of agricultural produce are subject to the Sale of Goods Act 1979, which lays down the basic legal rules on sales of goods generally. Amongst other things, the Act sets out certain conditions as to quality which are taken to be included in each contract for the sale of goods. (The seller's right to contract out is dealt with later.)

The conditions are:

(a) goods sold by description must match that description, even if the customer selects the goods. For example, in a self-service shop or a pick-your-own scheme any eggs or fruit sold must be of the size or variety offered on the label or notice and it makes no difference that the customer selects or picks the produce for himself.

(b) goods sold must be of "merchantable quality". This means that they must be as suitable for the purpose (or purposes) for which goods of the kind are commonly bought as it is reasonable to expect, considering the description used, the price and all other relevant circumstances. For example, apples sold as "dual purpose" must be suitable both for cooking and as dessert apples. Dairy produce should normally keep in a refrigerator for a short period of time but, if the price has been reduced for a quick sale, this indicates that the final date for consumption might be close and the produce cannot be expected to keep.

This condition does not apply if, before the goods are bought, the cause of complaint is specifically drawn to the customer's attention or he examines the goods and should see the defect of which he complains. Thus a customer normally has no legal cause for complaint that he was sold overripe fruit, if it was sold loose and he picked out the ones he wanted.

(c) if the customer makes known a particular purpose for which goods are required, they must be suitable for that purpose, except where he does not rely on the seller's skill or judgement or it is unreasonable to do so. So, if a customer in a farm shop says that he wants produce for freezing and, on the seller's advice, buys things which cannot be frozen satisfactorily, then the seller is liable for breach of condition. But, if the customer does not take the advice offered or the seller declines to give any, there is no cause for complaint when the produce bought proves to be unsuitable for the special purpose.

(d) where goods are sold by sample,
  (i) the bulk must correspond with the sample in quality.
  (ii) the customer must have a reasonable opportunity of comparing the two.
  (iii) the goods must be free from any defect rendering them unmerchantable which would not be apparent on reasonable examination of the sample.

The Unfair Contract Terms Act 1977 restricts the seller's right to contract out of these conditions by, for example, putting up notices stating that he does not accept liability.

(a) where the customer is dealing as "a consumer", any clause excluding or restricting the supplier's liability for breach of any of the implied terms is totally void.
(b) where the customer is dealing in any other capacity, any such clause is effective only in so far as it satisfies "the requirement of reasonableness".

A person "deals as consumer" if he is not acting in the course of business, but the other party to the contract is, and if the goods are of a type ordinarily supplied for private use. This usually applies in the case of direct sales to the public but might not in exceptional cases, as where the customer buys for catering purposes.

"The requirement of reasonableness" is satisfied where to contract out of liability was fair and reasonable in the circumstances known to the parties at the time of sale. Regard must also be had to:

(a) the relative bargaining positions of the parties;
(b) whether the customer received an inducement (such as a favourable price) to agree to the clause or could have bought the goods elsewhere without having to accept a similar clause;
(c) whether the customer knew the seller was contracting out;
(d) where the liability is excluded or restricted if some requirement (such as any complaint must be made on the day of purchase) is not met, whether it was reasonable to expect the customer to comply;

(e) whether the goods were specially produced or adapted for the customer.

All of the implied terms mentioned above are called "conditions". In general, the statutory implied terms are either "conditions" or "warranties".

On the breach of a condition by the supplier the customer can reject the goods, treat the contract as repudiated and recover any price paid. This applies unless the customer has waived the condition, has chosen to treat the breach as one of warranty, or has "accepted" the goods.

A breach of warranty merely entitles the customer to damages.

The point about the customer "accepting" the goods is that, if he wishes to reject them, he must promptly return them or, at least, notify the supplier that he is rejecting them. If the customer consumes the goods or keeps them for some time after finding a defect, he cannot then purport to reject them. In that case he can only treat the breach as one of a warranty and claim damages.

The effect of these rules is that a customer who buys defective food or other goods on a direct sale usually has a contractual right to complain and obtain redress. Normally the customer returns the defective goods and is refunded the price or is given replacement goods.

## 2.5 Consumer Protection Act 1987

This act covers consumer safety. It imposes strict liability on producers and manufacturers for defects in their products which cause damage to consumers. Where there is strict liability a consumer can claim against the producer without having to prove negligence.

But the Act specifically excludes primary agricultural produce. It does not apply to products of the soil, stock farming or fisheries which have not undergone an industrial process.

Whilst it remains to be seen exactly how this will be interpreted, the Act will not generally apply to raw agricultural produce normally sold in a farm shop or pick-your-own enterprise. However, if the produce has been processed in any way, liability might arise under the Act. The Act may therefore apply to items like sausages, meat pies, sliced vegetables, stewed or pureed fruit and dairy produce.

Although the strict liability provisions of the Act do not apply to primary agricultural produce, a farmer may be liable for damage to consumers where he has been negligent, for example, in breaching hygiene regulations. (See para. 2.7.)

## 2.6 Food Safety Act 1990

The Food Safety Act 1990 replaced much of the Food Act 1984, including the Milk and Dairy Regulations. The Act is enabling in nature, meaning that where food safety is threatened or consumers' interests are prejudiced, regulations may be made.

The Act controls the content, preparation and sale of food for human consumption. Amongst other things, it gives Ministers power to make regulations relating to food hygiene, novel foods and processes, the regulation of food premises and the training of all food handlers.

There are four key offences in the Act. The offences are rendering food injurious to health, offering for sale and/or possessing with the intention of sale, food failing to comply with food safety requirements, offering for sale food not of the nature, substance or quality demanded and falsely or misleadingly describing food.

Therefore, all farmers and growers must make sure that the output they offer for sale in whatever form does not contravene these offences. On successful prosecution the maximum penalties for cases tried in a Crown Court are unlimited fines and/or 2 years imprisonment. While in a Magistrates Court the maximum penalties are £20,000 fine and/or 6 months imprisonment.

This being the case it is important for farmers and growers to note the change in legal defences. Statutory warranties have been replaced by the "due diligence" defence. This makes two requirements of farmers and growers.

Firstly, *all* farmers and growers must show that they have in place and take *all reasonable precautions* to prevent the commission of an offence.

## 2.7 Hygiene

It is in the interests of every farmer and particularly those with a farm shop or roadside stall that he and his staff keep the highest standards of hygiene and cleanliness. It is both common and good business sense. The Food Safety Act 1990 and the amended Food Hygiene Regulations lay down important standards for cleanliness of premises and equipment used in a food business, the hygienic handling of food, and the cleanliness of people handling food.

Many of these requirements will apply to farm shops and some to those packing and storing eggs, fruit or vegetables. Any farmer who is slaughtering or butchering livestock on his premises, including the preparation of oven-ready poultry, will have to comply with a wide range of regulations which are not covered in this document. He should approach the Public Health Department of his local authority for further information.

The provisions of the Food Hygiene (General) Regulations 1990 are outlined below.

Therefore, good business practice must be followed such as checking inputs, applying all fertilisers, disinfectants and pest control substances according to the requirements of manufacturers' labels (Food and Environment Protection Act 1985) and taking measures to ensure that weighing equipment is operated correctly and labels do not mislead consumers.

Secondly, these measures in place, farmers and growers must keep accurate, up-to-date and presentable records of purchases, applications, batch numbers, employment training and other information which may enhance a legal defence for a period of 5 years. The checking process is acting with *due diligence*.

The Act gives enforcement authorities the power to inspect food premises, business records and food, seize food, serve

**23**

improvement notices, prohibition orders and emergency prohibition notices and orders.

It sets out the powers of entry and the procedures for the sampling and analysis of foodstuffs. It also allows for statutory Codes of Practice for its enforcement. Finally, the Act gives Ministers the authority to serve emergency control orders.

(a) From 1st April 1991 all foods covered by the Regulations as amended in 1990, must be kept at a temperature below 8 degrees centigrade. The foods covered are smoked or cured fish, soft cheeses, cooked products, smoked or cured meat which has been cut or sliced after smoking or curing, desserts (an ingredient of which is milk or anything used as a substitute for milk), prepared vegetable salads, cooked pies and pastries, cooked sausage rolls, uncooked or partly cooked pastry and dough products containing meat, fish and any substance used as a substitute for meat and fish, sandwiches and cream cakes.

From 1st April 1993 the foods which are most at risk of contamination with listeria must be kept at or below 8 degrees centigrade. These are foods which are eaten without further cooking.

From 1st April 1992 small delivery vehicles (less than 7.5 tonnes gross weight) will be required to deliver foods in the controlled categories within the 8 degree centigrade limit. Small vehicles making local deliveries will be exempt from the 8 degree centigrade requirement.

(b) "Food business" means any trade or business in which anyone handles food.

(c) "Food premises" means any building and any forecourt, yard or place of storage used in connection with the building, which houses a food business or from which a food business operates.

(d) "Food room" means any room in such premises in which anyone handles food.

**General requirements and the handling of food.**
Amongst other matters, the regulations covering the condition of food premises, handling of food and hygiene of food handlers, state:

1. A food business must not be carried on at any insanitary premises or place, or where the condition, situation or construction of any premises is such that food would be exposed to the risk of contamination.

2. Articles and equipment with which food is likely to come into contact must be kept clean and in good condition. All containers must be protected and kept free from contamination.

3. No food must be placed lower than 18 in from the ground unless it is adequately protected from the risk of contamination. Open food must be kept covered or effectively screened while exposed for sale.

4. Animal feed must not be kept in any room used for food handling unless it is in a container which will protect the food from the risk of contamination.

5. Any person who handles the food must take all reasonable steps necessary to protect the food from risk of contamination and must keep separate any food which is unfit for human consumption.

6. Any person who handles the food must:
   (a) keep all those parts of his person or clothing which are likely to come into contact with the food as clean as possible;
   (b) keep any open cut or abrasion on any exposed part of his person covered with a suitable waterproof dressing; and
   (c) refrain from spitting, and the use of tobacco and snuff, when handling, or in a room with, open food.

7. Food must not be carried in a container with any article which might contaminate it unless all reasonably practicable precautions are taken to avoid it doing so. Live animals and poultry must not come into contact with food. All wrapping paper, materials and containers must be clean. Printed material, unless designed for wrapping, must only be used for uncooked vegetables, unskinned rabbits or hares or unplucked game or poultry.

8. Anyone who becomes aware that he is suffering from a salmonella, dysenteric or staphylococcal infection likely to cause food poisoning must inform his employer or the

**25**

## 2 Legal Requirements

Medical Officer of Health at the local authority.

9. A sufficient supply of clean water must be provided at the premises. The local authority has power to exempt persons from this requirement.

**Requirements for premises from which food is sold.** There are numerous regulations covering food premises. The more important are, briefly:

(a) no vent pipe for drainage systems may be situated in food rooms and any inlets into such systems must be trapped.

(b) no cistern for the supply of water to a food room must supply a lavatory as well, except through an efficient flushing system.

(c) every lavatory used in connection with the premises must be properly lit and ventilated, and kept clean and in efficient order. It must not connect directly with the food room, or be sited where offensive smells can get into a food room. A notice must be placed in the lavatory requesting that people wash their hands after use.

(d) all food premises must have suitable and efficient hand basins in a convenient position, with an adequate supply of hot and cold water, soap and towels etc. If no open food is being handled only cold water is required. The hand basins must be kept clean and in good repair.

(e) sufficient supply of bandages, waterproof dressings and antiseptic must be kept in a readily accessible place.

(f) storage must be provided for staff clothing which is not being worn while handling food. The local authority may give exemption to this requirement.

(g) where open food is being handled there must be sufficient sink or other washing facilities for any necessary washing of food and equipment. If the sink is used only for the washing of fish, fruit or vegetables, no hot water need be provided.

(h) every food room must be suitably and sufficiently lit and, unless the humidity or temperature is controlled, it must have suitable and sufficient ventilation.

(i) all parts of every food room must be kept clean and in such condition that they can be effectively cleaned, and

**26**

any risk of infestation by rats, mice or insects prevented.
(j) refuse or filth must not be deposited or allowed to accumulate in a food room, except that which is unavoidable in the course of the business. Adequate space, suitably sited, must be provided for the removal of waste from food and for the separation of unfit food.
(k) a food room must not be used as a sleeping place and must not be used for handling open food if it is directly connected to a sleeping place. A local authority may give exemption to this requirement.

This summary is for guidance only. As substantial fines or even imprisonment are the penalty for failure to comply with the regulations it is important to consult the regulations or the local authority in your own case.

**The Food Hygiene (Markets, Stalls and Delivery Vehicles) Amendment Regulations 1966.** These regulations lay down basic food hygiene requirements in respect of markets, stalls and delivery vehicles. A "stall" includes any stand, marquee, tent, vehicle, vending machine, site or pitch from which food is sold. A delivery vehicle means any vehicle carrying food in the course of trade or business, but not any vehicle used for the sale of food.

Generally, all matters mentioned in the section entitled "General Requirements and the Handling of Food" above will apply to stalls. Certain requirements for premises may also apply where appropriate, and in particular (c), (d), (e), (g), (h) and (j) above. Other regulations for stalls and delivery vehicles include:

1. They must display the name and address of the person carrying on the business.
2. They shall not be used to store food unless the hygiene arrangements are satisfactory.
3. They must not be used as a sleeping place, unless, in the case of vehicles, there is an adequate partition separating the driving compartment from food.
4. Every stall selling unwrapped food, other than raw vegetables, must be suitably covered and screened at the back and sides and shall have adequate waste receptacles.

Some of the regulations will not apply to stores selling only covered food, and where the local authority has been notified in writing that unwrapped food is not being offered for sale. Some regulations do not apply to vending machines.

The way local authorities use their powers under these regulations can vary widely so it is particularly important that they should be consulted.

## 2.8 Weights and measures

The Weights and Measures Act 1985 controls the sale of goods by quantity or weight. Various regulations put specific restrictions on the sale of certain foodstuffs by quantity or weight. Regulations require certain foods to be sold in a particular way, for example pre-packed or in special containers. You are not allowed to sell goods in smaller quantities than stated on the package, or to misrepresent the quantity or weight of the goods in any way.

**Weighing and measuring equipment.** The Weights and Measures Act 1985 states that any weighing or measuring equipment used for trade must be passed as fit for use by a local weights and measures inspector, and, unless the equipment is too small, it must bear a stamp indicating that it has been passed. The stamp must not be defaced, except through fair wear and tear. The use of weighing or measuring equipment which has not been approved in the correct manner is punishable by a fine, and the equipment may be forfeited.

**Units of measurement.** The Weights and Measures Act 1985 states that in the United Kingdom, length should be measured in yards or metres, and mass in pounds or kilogrammes. A yard must be exactly 0.9144 metres, and a pound exactly 0.45359237 kilogrammes.

**Selling by weight or quantity.** The Act contains regulations covering the tolerances (i.e. margin of error) allowed in the sale of goods and the way the customer must be informed of the weight or quantity of the produce. The following paragraphs set out the broad requirements for a number of commodities, but it is important to remember that these are for guidance only and anyone selling produce should refer to the Act for the regulations covering the particular produce being sold as there are substantial penalties for those who fail to comply.

**"Countable produce"**. This term applies to foods which can be counted individually and includes apples, pears, peaches, cabbage, cauliflower, celery, cucumber, lettuce, onions, radishes and tomatoes.

**"Appropriate permitted weight"**. This refers to the weight of the containers which the Act permits to be used for various different products. The permitted weights of containers are set out in tables in the following paragraphs.

*Cheese, fish, meat\* and poultry*
(a) Prepacked Goods – These foods may only be sold prepacked if the net weight is marked on the container.

Except:
- Various cheeses set out in the regulations (including Cheddar, Cheshire, Derby, Double Gloucester, Leicestershire), whole Stilton cheese, cheese over 10 kg in weight, cheese under 25 g in weight, cheese packed in a container which does not exceed the permitted weight (*see Table 2.8.1*) provided the quantity is made known to the buyer before he pays for the goods;
- Goods sold in quantities of less than 5 g;
- Meat pies or poultry pies and sausage rolls.

(b) Unpacked Goods – These must be sold by net weight *or* if the container does not exceed the permitted weight, (*see Table 2.8.1*) they may be sold by net weight or gross weight.

Except:
- Meat pies or poultry pies or sausage rolls;

---

\*"Meat" in this context means any part of sheep, cattle or swine. It does not include horseflesh, venison or goatmeat. If in any doubt, check the weights and measures regulations.

- Goods sold in quantities less than 5 g;
- Cooked poultry, single cooked sausages;
- Shellfish;
- Cheese less than 25 g in weight.

| Gross weight of food and container | Permitted weight of container |
|---|---|
| Not exceeding 500 g | 5 g |
| Exceeding 500 g | 10 g per kg of the gross weight |

Table 2.8.1

*Fresh fruits and vegetables*
(excluding potatoes, soft fruit and mushrooms).

(a) Prepacked Goods – must be marked by net weight or, if countable produce, by number.

Except:
- Goods, prepacked with other goods in the same container;
- Vegetables sold in bunches (e.g. carrots, onions, parsley etc.)
- Food sold in quantities of under 5 g.

(b) Unpacked Goods – must be sold by net weight or, if countable produce, by number.

*Soft fruit and mushrooms*
These foods may be sold only:

(a) by net weight; or
(b) if the food is sold in a container which does not exceed the appropriate permitted weight (*see Table 2.8.2*), they may be sold by net or gross weight.

In either case the quantity must be made known to the buyer before he pays for the goods.

Except:
If the goods are packed with other goods in the same container.

| Gross weight of food and container | Permitted weight of container |
|---|---|
| Under 250 g | 120 g per kg of the gross weight |
| Over 250 g up to 1 kg | 100 g per kg of the gross weight |
| Over 1 kg up to 3 kg | 90 g per kg of the gross weight |
| Over 3 kg | 60 g per kg of the gross weight |

Table 2.8.2

*Fruit and vegetables divided into pieces*
These goods may only be sold by net weight, whether they are prepacked or not.

*Potatoes*
(a) Prepacked Goods – These must be sold in prescribed quantities of:
   – 8 oz, 12 oz, 1 lb, 1.5 lb, or a multiple of 1 lb;
   Or
   – 500 g, 1 kg, 1.5 kg, 2 kg, 2.5 kg or a multiple of 2.5 kg up to and including 15 kg, 20 kg or 25 kg.
   The weight must be marked on the container.
(b) Unpacked Goods – These must be sold by net weight or, if sold in a container which does not exceed the permitted weight (*see Table 2.8.3*), they may be sold either by net weight or gross weight.

| Gross weight of food and container | Permitted weight of container |
|---|---|
| Up to 500 g | 5 g |
| Over 500 g | 10 g per kg of the gross weight |

Table 2.8.3

*Milk*

Milk must only be sold by capacity measurement (e.g. pints or litres) or net weight unless bottled or otherwise prepacked.

If prepacked it must be sold in prescribed quantities of a third of a pint, half a pint, or multiple of half a pint;

Or

200 ml, 250 ml, 500 ml, 750 ml, 1 litre, 2 litres or multiples of 500 ml.

Vending machines selling milk must show the quantity clearly.

*Bread*

A whole loaf of bread over 300 g net weight must be sold in quantities of 400 g or a multiple of 400 g. There are no requirements where a loaf is less than 300 g.

*Eggs*

These must be sold by number and if prepacked, the container must be marked with the number of eggs it contains unless all the eggs can be seen by the purchaser, and it does not hold more than six eggs.

*Honey and jam*

These must be sold by net weight. If prepacked they must only be sold in the prescribed quantities of 2 oz, 4 oz, 8 oz, 12 oz, 1 lb, 1.5 lbs, or a multiple of 1 lb (unless sold in quantities of less than 50 g). Chunk honey and comb honey are exempt and can be sold in any quantity.

*Flour*

This must be sold by net weight. If prepacked it must be sold in prescribed quantities of 125 g, 250 g, 500 g or multiples of 500 g.

*Edible fats (including butter, margarine, dripping, lard)*

These must be sold by net weight. If prepacked they must be sold in prescribed quantities of 50 g, 125 g, 250 g, 500 g or multiples of 500 g, up to 4 kg, and thereafter in multiples of 1 kg up to 10 kg.

## 2.9 Labelling and advertising of food

The food labelling regulations are important to farmers and growers, both those who sell produce at the farm gate direct to the consumer and those who sell through other outlets. The main legislation is the Food Labelling Regulations 1984, but other legislation can affect the marking and advertisement of produce, including the Trade Descriptions Act 1968 and the Weights and Measures Legislation.

**Price Marking Order 1991**. Price Marking Orders will apply to most produce. Under the Price Marking Order 1991 the seller must indicate to the customer the price of food.

If the food is sold by reference to quantity as to a unit of measurement then unit pricing must be given or a price given for each multiple of units in which the food is sold. A number of foodstuffs are exempt from unit pricing; goods sold by number or in a bunch, an assortment of different items sold in a single pack of goods (e.g. soup mix), prepared dishes and goods contained in a single pack of goods from which a mixture is to be prepared, a portion of meat or poultry cut at the request of, and in the presence of, an intending customer, perishable food sold at reduced prices on account of the danger of its deterioration and food sold from bulk or food prepacked in variable quantities where the quantity is less than 50 g or 50 ml, or is more than 10 kg or 10 litres.

The price of goods must be unambiguous and marked clearly, and must be easily seen by customers at the sales selection point. A comprehensive price list is permitted instead of posting individual prices adjacent to each item. The marking of unit pricing must be on or adjacent to the goods, or if the goods are prepacked, on or adjacent to the containers or both.

The Price Marking Order 1991 will retain the requirements of previous Marking Orders for cheese and meat. Therefore prepacked cheese and meat must be unit priced if the weight is marked on the container, usually in terms of prices per kilogramme or pound.

It is good trading practice for all produce sold to be price marked.

## 2  Legal Requirements

**General labelling requirement.** The name of any food not prepacked, or which is prepacked for direct sale (i.e. prepacked by the retailer on the premises) must be on the label. Certain unusual foods have correct names fixed by law in the regulations. These do not normally apply to farm produce, but the species or variety of melons and potatoes must be marked.

Prepacked foods (not prepacked by the retailer for direct sale) must be marked or labelled with the following:

1. The name of the food.
2. A list of ingredients – listed in descending order of weight. The following foods need not list ingredients: fresh fruit and vegetables, cheese, butter, fermented milk or cream, flour, vinegar.
3. The Food Labelling (Amendment) Regulations 1990 require from January 1991 "use by" dates on microbiologically perishable food whilst "best before" dates remain for the majority of other foods. The "sell by" date is no longer permitted. There are separate Regulations dealing with eggs and poultry.
4. Any special storage conditions.
5. The name or business name and address of the manufacturer or packer.
6. The place of origin of the food, if failure to give this may mislead the purchaser.
7. Instructions for use where needed.

The general labelling rules do not apply to honey, hen eggs or milk but do cover cream and food containing milk.

**Additive declaration.** The labelling of foods whether prepacked or not must mention the presence of such things as additives, preservatives, antioxidants, artificial sweeteners, colours, flavour enhancers, or flavourings.

The following are exempted from this:

1. Foods sold in packages of less than 10 square centimetres in area.
2. Fresh fruit and vegetables which have not been peeled and cut into pieces.

34

3.  Cheese, butter, fermented milk and fermented cream. Flour.

**Irradiated food.** The Food (Control of Irradiation) Regulations 1990 permit the sale of irradiated food. The Food Labelling (Amendment) (Irradiated Food) Regulations 1990 require that all irradiated food is labelled "irradiated" or "treated with ionising radiation".

These regulations also require that all the listed ingredients which have been irradiated must be indicated in compound foods and food sold by caterers either on the premises or for consumption elsewhere.

**Intoxicating liquor.** The Food Labelling (Amendment) Regulations 1989 mean that all prepacked alcoholic drinks other than Community controlled wine with an alcoholic strength greater by volume than 1.2% shall be marked or labelled with an indication of its alcoholic strength by volume in the form of a figure to not more than one decimal place immediately before the symbol %vol. Similarly, where alcoholic drinks are sold other than prepacked the alcoholic strength must be displayed.

**Tenderised meat.** Meat, whether prepacked or not, which has been treated with proteolytic enzymes or comes from animals so treated may not be sold unless the word "tenderised" appears as part of the name on the label.

**Milk.** The Milk and Milk Products (Protection of Designations) Regulations 1990 mean that with the exception of cows' milk all other food products cannot use the name "milk" or any other word or description which implies the food contains milk unless the actual product has all the normal constituents in their natural proportions, the name of the animal from which the milk is sourced is stated and any processes to which the milk has been subjected are stated.

The Milk (Special Designation) Regulations 1989 require that unpasteurised milk carries the following declaration:

"This milk has not been heat treated and may therefore contain organisms harmful to health."

It is likely that labelling requirements for unpasteurised cheese will be made in 1991.

**Ungraded eggs.** The Ungraded Eggs (Hygiene) Regulation 1990 makes it an offence to sell to a person buying other than for the purpose of re-sale (excluding caterers for the purpose of his catering business and/or a manufacturer for the purpose of his manufacturing business) any egg which contains a crack visible without handling to the naked eye.

**Claims made about foodstuff.** The Food Labelling Regulations ban claims as to the special benefits to be derived from eating particular foods. Some claims may be made in accordance with conditions set out in the regulations, as with the cover claims about the energy, calorie, protein, vitamin or mineral content of the food, and slimming, health or diabetic benefits. It is most important to refer to the detailed regulations when making any such claims. (Food Labelling Regulations 1984, Regulation 36 and Schedule 6.)

**General requirements as to the manner of marking or labelling food.** All marking and labelling must be:

1.  Clearly legible, easy to understand and indelible.
2.  In a conspicuous position, easily seen, either on the food or close to it.
3.  Uninterrupted and not hidden or obscured by any other written or pictorial matter.
4.  If the food has to be marked or labelled to indicate net quantity or minimum durability, these markings must be placed within the same field of vision as the name of the food.
5.  Any list of ingredients should be right next to the name of the food and no particular ingredient should stand out.
6.  The labelling must not mislead the purchaser in any way about the nature, substance, or quality of the food.

**Size of letters on containers.** The height of letters for the name of the food must be:

(a) for a container under 12 cm, at least 2 mm.
(b) for containers between 12 and 30 cm, at least 3 mm.
(c) for containers between 30 and 45 cm, at least 4 mm.
(d) for containers over 45 cm, at least 6 mm.

The name of the food must be more prominent than any other information which must be given.

**Trade Descriptions Act 1968.** This Act makes it an offence in the course of a trade or business, to apply a false trade description to any goods or to supply any goods with a false trade description (e.g. it is an offence to sell battery-produced eggs as free range eggs). It is also an offence to give false or misleading indications as to the price of goods.

A person "applies" a trade description if he affixes or annexes it to goods, or marks it on, or incorporates it with goods, or anything with which they are supplied, or otherwise uses a description which is likely to be taken as referring to the goods.

**Other regulations.** It is important to refer to price marking and weights and measures regulations as certain goods must be marked with a price and the net or gross weight.

Note these notes are for guidance only. They do not give a comprehensive list of all the regulations. There are substantial penalties for failure to comply with regulations so if you are in doubt, check the regulations themselves or contact the appropriate local authority.

# 2.10 Health, safety and welfare of employees

Employers have long been legally obliged to take reasonable care over the safety of their employees, and this includes employees in farm shops and other direct sales points.

Employers also have to observe many statutory provisions covering the safety, health and welfare of their employees. Employers not doing so are liable to criminal prosecution, as well as to civil claims by the employee in damages. The main statutes of importance to direct selling enterprises are:

Health and Safety at Work etc. Act 1974
Offices, Shops and Railway Premises Act 1963
Agriculture (Safety, Health and Welfare Provisions) Act 1956
Shops Act 1950.

**Offices, Shops and Railway Premises Act 1963.** In general this Act applies to all places where retail trade is carried on, including sales of meals or refreshment. The Act covers the health, safety and welfare of employees, over such matters as ventilation, cleanliness, lavatories, the safety of floors, temperature, lighting and washing facilities.

Local authorities (district councils) are responsible for enforcing the Act and should be consulted on the detailed requirements.

**Agriculture (Safety, Health and Welfare Provisions) Act 1956.** In some circumstances, an employee involved in a direct selling enterprise other than in a farm shop will be covered by this Act. The Act contains measures to protect young employees and to avoid accidents to children and also enables the Health and Safety Executive to insist that lavatories and washing facilities are provided.

**Health and Safety at Work etc. Act 1974.** This Act also has provisions applicable to agricultural workers. It lays down the general duty of employers to ensure the health, safety and welfare at work of employees, as far as practicable.

The Act also established the Health and Safety Executive as an enforcement authority. Regulations and Codes of Practice under the Act will eventually replace most of the other legislation on health, safety and welfare.

**Shops Act 1950.** This is covered by chapter 2.12.

**Insurance.** All employers must now have adequate insurance to cover personal injuries to employees whilst at work, under the Employers Liability (Compulsory Insurance) Act 1969 and Employers Liability (Defective Equipment) Act 1969. Consult your NFU Group Secretary for details of suitable policies.

## 2.11 Safety of visitors

A farmer or grower operating a direct selling enteprise might have visitors on his land or premises who are there as customers. This applies, for example, if he has a farm shop or runs a pick-your-own enterprise.

Under the Occupier's Liability Acts 1957 and 1984 an owner occupier or tenant may be liabile to pay damages to a visitor who is injured due to the defective or dangerous state of his land or premises. He must make sure that his premises are not dangerous to visitors by, for example, seeing that repairs are carried out when necessary and that any hazards are isolated, and warnings posted.

Children need special attention. They are likely to be attracted to such things as farm machinery left in or near a field where pick-your-own activities are organised, or near a farm shop. If children are injured when playing on such machinery the farmer will be liable. It is important to remember that children will explore where adults would not be expected to go.

It is vital to insure against the risk of injury to visitors, so consult your NFU Group Secretary before setting up the new venture.

## 2.12 Shop closing hours

Farm shops, like any others are subject to certain regulations controlling opening hours. The Shops Acts 1950 to 1965 control the hour at which a shop must close. A shop is defined in the 1950 Act as "any premises where any retail trade or business is carried on", and this will include farm shops and pick-your-own enterprises.

As a general rule every shop has to be closed for the serving of customers by 9 o'clock in the evening on the late day and by 8 o'clock in the evening on any other day of the week.

The late day will be Saturday unless the local authority, by order, fixes some other day. The local authority may also vary the closing hour by "a closing order", though the hour fixed should not be earlier than 7 o'clock in the evening.

The Acts provide that every shop shall have an early closing day on one week day in every week. However, shops selling meat, fish, milk, cream, bread, confectionary, fruit, vegetables, flowers and other articles of a perishable nature are exempt.

Generally, a farm shop may open from early morning to 8 or 9 o'clock in the evening. It may also open for the sale of home-grown produce on Sundays.

Local authorities may fix special closing hours for shops in their areas, so it is wise to consult them when setting up a new retail venture.

## 2.13 Sunday trading

The Shops Act 1950 makes it an offence to sell any goods on a Sunday with certain exceptions, including the following:

1.   Flowers, fresh fruit and fresh vegetables.
2.   Milk and cream, other than tinned or dried milk or cream but including clotted cream even if sold in tins.
3.   Newly cooked provisions.

These goods may be sold from a shop (including a farm shop) or any other place of sale on a Sunday.

A farmer or horticulturist may also sell any other home grown produce on a Sunday at his farm or smallholding, but such sales must not be from a "shop". A shop in this context means a building or some permanent structure as opposed to vehicles or temporary stalls. Thus a farmer producing, for example, fresh vegetables and eggs, can sell the vegetables from his farm shop on a Sunday, but he cannot sell the eggs from the shop. He could sell the eggs from, for example, a stall.

There is no statutory definition for the term "home-grown produce" and farmers and horticulturalists have had problems trading on Sundays. For example, some local authorities have interpreted the term very strictly and have forbidden the sale of plants in containers on Sundays as the containers are not "home-grown". This interpretation is extreme but you may be breaking the law if you sell anything other than home-grown produce on Sundays and you may need special permission from the local authority.

Following a European Court Ruling in November 1989 on the compatibility of the Shops Act 1950 and the Treaty of Rome Article that deals with quantitative restrictions on imports and all measures having equivalent effect, the English Courts have been left in a state of confusion over the question of prosecuting those who breach the Sunday Trading Laws. Each case will be considered on its own special facts.

However, it should be borne in mind that in cases of persistent flouting of the 1950 Act the Local Authority can obtain a Civil Injunction to prevent an enterprise trading on a Sunday, without the need for them to obtain a prior successful conviction.

**Local authority bye-laws.** Certain local authorities are entitled to make bye-laws relating to Sunday trading. These bye-laws may cover such matters as the length of time a shop may be open; allowing the sale of goods including food, photo requisites, souvenirs, photographic reproductions and postcards in circumstances where recreational facilities are being provided (limited to not more than 18 Sundays in any year); and making partial exemption orders on Sundays for the sale of goods commonly sold in a grocery shop. It is important to check whether bye-laws exist if you are considering opening on a Sunday.

**Deliveries.** Generally, it is an offence to make deliveries from a shop on a Sunday unless Christmas Eve or Christmas Day should fall on a Sunday.

## 2.14 "Pick-your-own" selling

The number of pick-your-own enterprises has grown rapidly over the last few years and anyone starting such a business must consider the legal requirements. As a general rule, it is safe to assume that the planning and other regulations for farm shops also apply to pick-your-own operations.

**Planning matters.** The sale of produce on a pick-your-own basis will, by definition, mean the sale from a holding of its unprocessed produce. So there will be no definite change of use and no planning permission is needed to set it up.

**Labelling.** All goods and produce must be correctly labelled. Prepacked goods must be labelled in a specific manner set down in the labelling regulations. The price must be clearly displayed in a prominent position if not marked on the produce itself (*see pages 33–37*).

**Hygiene.** The premises must meet the standards set in the hygiene regulations (*see pages 23–28*).

**Weights and measures.** Any weighing equipment must be passed as fit for use by a local Weights and Measures inspector under the Weights and Measures Act 1985, unless the equipment is too small to be stamped and marked.

**Occupier's liability.** Under the Occupier's Liability Acts 1957 and 1984 the occupier of land may be liable for a civil claim in damages in the event of any accident or injury suffered by a third party on his land. He is under a duty to ensure that all practical and reasonable steps are taken to isolate any dangers and warn persons on the land of those dangers. He has a duty to anyone invited on to the land, and, in certain circumstances, the duty may extend to trespassers.

Adequate insurance cover is therefore vital and practicable steps should be taken to isolate dangers. Remember that children will frequently be coming onto the land with their parents, and this necessitates a higher standard of care on your part.

When undertaking a pick-your-own enterprise it is important to consider:

– Will the activity involve a material change of the land?
– Do you have adequate facilities, e.g. parking, access?

- If not, will you require planning permission?
- Are the premises safe? Have obstacles been removed and dangers isolated?
- Do warning signs need to be erected?
- Has your weighing equipment been passed as fit for use and stamped?
- Is the produce correctly labelled?
- Have you complied with hygiene regulations?
- Have you checked with the local authority to ensure that local bye-laws are not being breached?

## 2.15 Rating

The Local Government Finance Act 1988 section 51 (Schedule 5) provides that agricultural land and agricultural buildings are exempt from non-domestic rating.

Agricultural land is defined as including, inter alia, "anything which consists of a market garden, nursery ground, orchard or allotment...".

This applies to land used to grow fruit and other crops, even if the public are permitted onto the land to pick them. However, a problem does arise in the case of nursery stock, particularly container-grown plants, since these may very often either be brought onto a holding relatively shortly before sale, or moved from one part of the holding to an open sales area. In these cases the land is likely to be subject to rates. But where plants are "grown on" to a significant degree, whether in containers or not, and the public nevertheless have access for the purpose of choosing plants to purchase, it can be argued that rates should not apply. There has been no test case to decide where the line should be drawn. But a reasonable test is probably whether the main use of any particular area of land is to grow stock or to display it for sale.

An agricultural building is defined as, inter alia, "not a dwelling and it is occupied together with agricultural land..." or "it is or forms part of a market garden" and in either case it "is used solely in connection with agricultural operations..." on the land or at the market garden.

Farm shops are considered rateable since, in the view of the Inland Revenue, they constitute a separate commercial undertaking.

A recent court decision confirmed that this is true in most cases where farm shops, even if only selling the produce of the holding upon which they stand, set aside part of a building for the sole purpose of retail sales, advertise the existence of the shop and keep it open for specified hours although it may not be throughout the year. It is considered then that the purpose of the shop is the retail sale of produce and is not part of an agricultural operation.

A similar problem arises with land on which nursery stock is grown/displayed in connection with glass-houses which are sometimes used both for growing container plants and at the same time for their display for sale. Your best course of action on holdings of this type is to make sure that sales areas and growing areas are clearly identified and demarcated.

However, other areas such as car parks will probably be liable to rates. This will apply even where the car park is grassland, since the agricultural land exemption requires the land to be used as meadow or pasture ground "only" and use as a car park, even for a part of the year, may render it liable for rates.

# 3. Appendices

## Appendix I: Acts and regulations

The following are the more important Acts and Regulations which control aspects of the direct selling of agricultural produce:

Building Regulations, 1985
Consumer Protection Act, 1987
Food Hygiene (Markets, Stalls and Delivery Vehicles) Regulations, 1966
Food Hygiene (General) Regulations, 1970 (as amended)
Food Labelling Regulations, 1990
Food Safety Act, 1990
Health and Safety at Work etc. Act, 1974
Milk and Dairies (General) Regulations, 1959 (as amended)
Milk (Special Designation) Regulations, 1989 (as amended)
Occupier's Liability Act, 1957
Occupier's Liability Act, 1984
Offices, Shops and Railway Premises Act, 1963
Price Marking Order, 1990
Sale of Goods Act, 1979
Shops Acts, 1950–1965
The Control of Roadside Sales Order (Procedure) Regulations, 1978
Town and Country Planning Act, 1990
Town and Country Planning (Agricultural and Forestry Development in National Parks etc.) Special Development Order, 1988
Town and Country Planning (Control of Advertisements) Regulations, 1989
Town and Country Planning (Fees for Applications and Deemed Applications) Regulations, 1983
Town and Country Planning (Fees for Applications and Deemed Applications) (Amendment) Regulations, 1985
Trade Descriptions Act, 1968
Weights and Measures Act, 1963 (Cheese, Fish, Fresh Fruits and Vegetables, Meat and Poultry) Order 1984

Weights and Measures Act, 1963 (Miscellaneous Foods) Order 1984

Weights and Measures Act, 1985

**Local acts and bye-laws.** In addition it should be borne in mind that some county councils have obtained special powers in relation to roadside selling by way of Private (or Local) Acts of Parliament. Local authorities also have statutory powers to make bye-laws covering food shops, food sales and roadside selling. It is therefore important before starting a business to check whether any local acts or bye-laws which relate to starting a business apply to you.

# Appendix II: Sources of further advice and information

## 1. Rural Enterprise Advisors

*East*

Mr. W. Johnson
Ministry of Agriculture
Block C
Brooklands Avenue
Cambridge
CB2 2DR
Telephone (0223) 358911

*South East*

Terry Bradfield
Block A
Government Offices
Coley Park
Reading
RG1 6DI
Telephone (0734) 581222

*South West*

Mr. Graham Pugh
Ministry of Agriculture
Burdgehill Road
Westbury on Tryn
Bristol BS10 6NJ
Telephone (0272) 591000

*Midlands and Western*

Mr. P. R. Dart
Woodthorne
Wolverhampton
WV6 8TQ
Telephone (0902) 754190

*Northern*

Mr. K. G. Kingston
Block 2
Government Buildings
Lawnswood
Leeds LS16 6PY
Telephone (0532) 611223

*Wales*

Mr. D. T. D. Davis
Trawscoed
Aberystwyth
Dyfed
SY23 4HT
Telephone (09743) 301

### 3 Appendices

## 2. MAFF

17 Smith Square
London
SW1P 3JR
Telephone (071) 238 5642

## 3. Farm Shop and Pick Your Own Association

NFU
Agricultural House
Knightsbridge
London
W1X 7NJ
Telephone (071) 235 5077
Contact: Jane Connor, Secretary

FSPA provide specialist services to farm shop owners including publicity material, a monthly magazine and it also has a code of conduct for its members.

## 4. NFU Membership Services

4 St. Mary's Hill
Stamford
Lincs
PE9 2DP
Telephone (0780) 51513

# Index

Additives, 34
Advertisements, 3, 13
Advertising Standards Authority, 3
Agriculture (Safety, Health and Welfare Provisions) Act 1956, 38
"Appropriate permitted weight", 29
Areas of outstanding natural beauty, 16
Areas of special control, 15

Bread, weight, 32
Building Act 1984, 18
Building control, 17
Building operations, 6

Chambers of Commerce, 2
Change of use, 7
Children, safety of, 39
"Closing order", 39
Conservation Areas, 16
Consumer Protection Act 1987, 21
Containers
    size of letters on, 37
    weight of, 29
"Countable produce", 29

Delivery vehicles, 24
Department of Trade and Industry, 3
Design Advisory Service, 3
Design Council, 4
Development Rights, removal of, 7
"Due diligence", 22, 23

Edible fats, weight, 32
Eggs, quantity, 32
Employees, 37
Employers Liability (Compulsory Insurance) Act 1969, 38
Employers Liability (Defective Equipment) Act 1969, 38
Engineering operations, 7
Enterprise Agencies, 2

# Index

Farm diversification scheme, 3
Farm Shop and Pick Your Own Association, 48
Fish, 9
Flour, weight, 32
"Food business", definition of, 24
Food Hygiene (General) Regulations 1990, 23
Food Hygiene (Markets, Stalls and Delivery Vehicles) Amendment
   Regulations 1966, 27
Food Labelling Regulations 1990, 34
"Food premises" definition of, 24
Food premises, regulations covering, 26
"Food room", definition of, 24
Food Safety Act 1990, 22
Fresh fruits and vegetables, weight, 30
Fruit, 10
Fruit and vegetables divided into pieces, weight, 31

General development orders, 6

Handling of food, 24
Health and Safety at Work etc. Act 1974, 38
Health and Safety Executive, 38
Honey and jam, weight, 32
Horticultural produce, 10
Hygiene, 23

Inland Revenue, 44
Insurance, 4
Intoxicating liquor, 35
Irradiated food, 35

Labelling, 33, 42
Libraries, 2
Local authority bye-laws, 41, 46
Local Government Finance Act 1988, 43

MAFF, 3, 48
Margins of error, 28
Market research, 1
Measuring equipment, 28
Meat, 9
   tenderised, 35

"Merchantable quality", definition of, 19
Milk
    quantity, 32
Milk and milk products, 9, 35

National Parks, 12
    advertising in, 16
New buildings, erection of, 17
NFU Membership Services, 3, 48

Occupier's Liability Acts, 42
Offices, Shops and Railway Premises Act 1963, 38
"Open food", 25

"Pick your own" selling, 41
Planning fees, 12
Planning permission, 6, 11, 12
Post Office, 4
Potatoes, weight, 31
Poultry, 9
Prepacked goods, 29
Price Marking Order 1991, 33
Profit targets, 3
Promotion, 3
Public Health Deparment, 23

Rates, 43
"Requirement of reasonableness", 20
Retail margins, 2
Retail skills, 1
Rural Development Commission, 3
Rural Enterprise Advisors, 47

Safety of visitors, 39
Sale of Goods Act 1979, 18
Sale of home-grown produce, 8
Sale of produce not grown on holding, 8
Selling by weight or quantity, 28
Shop closing hours, 39
Shop layout, 4
Shops Act 1950, 39
Size of letters on containers, 37
Small Firms Services, 2

## Index

Soft fruit and mushrooms, weight, 30
Stalls, 27
Sunday trading, 40

Tenderised meat, 35
Tolerances, 28
Town and Country Planning Act 1990, 6
Town and Country Planning (Control of Advertisements) Regulations 1989, 13
Trade Descriptions Act, 37

Unfair Contract Terms Act 1977, 20
Ungraded Eggs (Hygiene) Regulation 1990, 36
Units of measurement, 28
Unpacked goods, 29
"Use by" dates, 34
"Use rules", application of, 7

Vegetables, 10
Visitors, safety of, 39

Weighing equipment, 28
Weights and Measures Act 1985, 28
Wine and cider, 10

# Are You a Member of the NFU?

If yes, then you are entitled to a 20% discount from Shaws' other titles as listed below. As up-to-date guides to legal problems faced by farmers, these books will be of great interest. All the books are written for the use of laymen, but with reference to law cases. Acts and Statutory Instruments are also available for those who require them.

All prices stated include postage and packing.

### Animal Law

A concise but comprehensive guide to legal aspects of ownership, theft, sale, import/export and movement of animals. Also covered are the law as relating to pets, farm and game animals, the protection of animals, diseases and pests.

Price £10.25.    20% NFU discount price £8.20
ISBN 0 7219 0801 2

### Countryside Law

A central theme in this book is the need to accommodate the competing demands to protect the countryside and also make use of its potential in terms of agricultural activity and recreation. Subjects covered include: protection and enjoyment of the countryside, planning, access, commons, protection of species and pollution.

Price TBA.
ISBN 0 7219 1061 0

### Guide to Angling Law

A clear, comprehensive explanation of fishery law, presented in a format which makes it an ideal source of information. Covering the law in England and Wales, and Scotland.

Price £9.95.    20% NFU discount price £7.96
ISBN 0 7219 1240 0

## Horse Law

A comprehensive legal guide to all aspects of ownership and responsibility, including buying and selling, riding stables, where riding is legally possible and rights of way, horses in sport and in hunting. Transport, insurance, breeding, protection and the registration of farriers are also covered.

Price £9.95.     20% NFU discount price £7.96
ISBN 0 7219 1130 7

## Law Relating to Mobile Homes and Caravans

This book gives a comprehensive outline of the law relating to caravans. The control of sites, planning permission and site licensing are covered. Use of caravans as homes and by gypsies are also explored fully.

Price £12.50.     20% NFU discount price £10.00
ISBN 0 7219 0811 X

## Your Dog and the Law

All aspects of the law relating to dogs for farmers are fully covered: ownership and theft, disease, trespassing, dangerous dogs, killing dogs, and dogs and game.

Price £4.95.     20% NFU discount price £3.96
ISBN 0 7219 1011 4

Send your order, with a cheque enclosed, post **free** addressed to:

SHAW & SONS LTD
**FREEPOST**
DARTFORD
DA1 4BR

**Please state your NFU Membership Card number as proof of NFU membership when making your order. Thank you.**